AIRFIX KITS

Trevor Pask

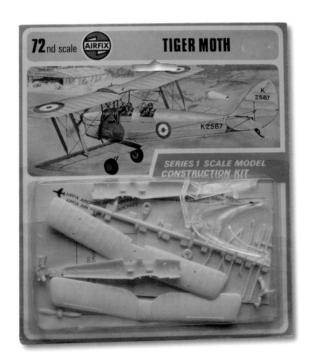

SHIRE PUBLICATIONS

Published in Great Britain in 2010 by Shire Publications Ltd,
Midland House, West Way, Botley, Oxford OX2 0PH,
United Kingdom.

44-02 23rd Street, Suite 219, Long Island City,
NY 11101, USA.

E-mail: shire@shirebooks.co.uk   www.shirebooks.co.uk

© 2010 Trevor Pask

A CIP catalogue record for this book is available from the
British Library.

Shire Library no. 598 . ISBN-13: 978 0 74780 791 9

Trevor Pask has asserted his right under the Copyright,
Designs and Patents Act, 1988, to be identified as the
author of this book.

Designed by Myriam Bell Design, France and typeset
in Perpetua and Gill Sans.
Printed in China through Worldprint Ltd.

10 11 12 13 14   10 9 8 7 6 5 4 3 2 1

COVER IMAGE
An Airfix advertisement from the 1975 catalogue.

TITLE PAGE IMAGE
The Tiger Moth kit in the short-lived 'blister' type
packaging used by Airfix in the mid 1970s.

CONTENTS PAGE IMAGE
Twenty-one years later the RAF's Jaguar fighters were
painted pale pink and fought in the first Gulf War, but in
1970 they had only just flown as prototypes. Airfix was
quick off the mark with a kit.

AUTHOR'S NOTE
With special thanks to Darell Burge of Hornby for being so
generous in allowing access to the image archive at
Hornby / Airfix, to Steven S. Pietrobon for advice and
imagery, to Peter van Lune for imagery, to Mario
Wens for imagery, to Dinke Austin for proofreading and
encouragement, and to my mother who bought me the first
kit but who sadly died a few months before this book was
completed. She often did not like the mess, but I am sure
she would have thought it was all worthwhile in the end!

Shire Publications is supporting the Woodland Trust, the UK's leading woodland conservation charity, by funding the dedication of trees.

CONTENTS

HOW THE 'AIRFIX KIT' CAME ABOUT

THERE HAVE BEEN MANY companies associated with plastic model kits, but perhaps the best known is Airfix. The term 'Airfix kit' has, in Britain at least, become the generic term for any plastic model, or anything assembled from separate components. While I was writing this book, the term 'like a gigantic Airfix kit' was used in two BBC news reports. One described the construction of the Apollo 11 rocket, and the other described the final assembly line of the A380 double-decker airliner. More subtle, but in the same vein, was the use of the Airfix brand by a bank in a major advertising campaign.

Clearly the media think that the British public know what an 'Airfix kit' is. Why this may be the case is easy to answer. There can be few people – and hardly any boys – born in the UK after the 1950s who have not experienced the joys or frustrations of building a plastic construction kit – a kit which during the 1960s and 1970s would almost certainly have been manufactured by Airfix.

Plastic model kits as we know them have existed since the late 1940s, and earlier variants since the 1930s. Models, however, have existed for much longer. The Romans were especially fond of miniature racing chariots and figures of gladiators – reflecting interests that were literally the equivalent of current day Formula One motor racing or Champions League soccer. However, until the nineteenth century when the first constructional toys such as building blocks appeared, models were sold as completed items or had to be made at home. Such home-made models varied from simple figures carved from scraps of wood to elaborate ships in bottles and miniature engineering replicas. Whatever the skill or time available to the model maker, the impulse to create a

Opposite and below: The box art and contents of the Frog Supermarine Spitfire kit from 1938. It was the first plastic kit ever produced of the Spitfire.

5

The box art and contents of the Frog Hawker Fury. The early Frog Penguins came complete with paints and cement.

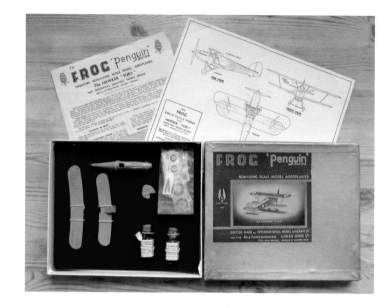

The Frog Penguin catalogue from 1938: the world's first range of plastic construction kits.

miniature seems to have been a constant human need. This need has sought a form in the available materials of the time: wood, stone, paper, clay, metal, and – a few decades into the twentieth century – plastic.

The first model kits that the modern eye would recognise were produced in the early 1930s by the British company Skybirds. These were 1:72 scale aircraft kits that helped the modeller along by providing the major components – the fuselages and wings – in balsa wood, which had been pre-cut and shaped. Hard-to-make items such as wheels, undercarriage legs, propellers and canopies were supplied as metal castings, or mouldings in one of the early synthetic materials such as acetate or Bakelite. These 'solid' kits were popular, and they survived until the 1950s, but they still required a high degree of skill and practice to achieve an acceptable result. The wooden components still had to be trimmed and sanded to achieve an accurate outline, and constant reference was needed to a set of scale drawings.

A more radical innovation was the Frog Penguin aircraft range from the late 1930s. Manufactured by International Model Aircraft, which was part of the Lines Brothers toy empire, Frog Penguin kits inherited their odd name from the company brand name, which came from 'Flies Right Off the Ground' (the slogan applied to all the company's flying models) and the flightless nature of the penguin. The Penguin kits were similar to the solid wooden kits, but the components were produced in cellulose acetate. Cellulose acetate is an unstable material that is prone to warping if cooled too quickly during manufacture. Despite this shortcoming, the material had the significant advantage of being able to provide the core components of a model without the need for cutting or sanding; at most some work to smooth over the small gaps between joints was required. Like modern kits, the Frog Penguins were also hollow, with the fuselage of an aircraft being moulded in two halves – although they often came glued together in the box to minimise the tendency of the material to warp. In most respects, these kits were the prototypes of the ones Airfix and other companies would later produce.

The technology that made the Frog Penguins possible was that of injection moulding. In theory this is a straightforward process whereby liquid material is injected into

Modelling of all types was a very popular hobby in the 1950s, when most real-life jobs involved making things. This Revell advertisement from March 1956 demonstrates the context into which the plastic kit was born: things are 'real', 'perfect', 'exciting' and 'scaled from original plans'.

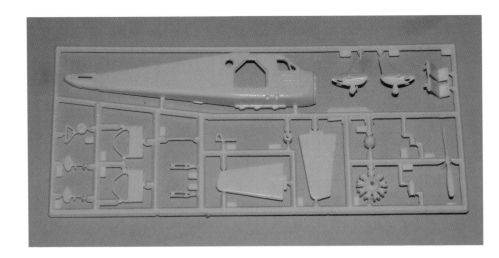

What comes out of the mould – the raw components of a kit. These good examples of Airfix's mould-making skills from the 1970s are the 1:72 de Havilland Beaver from 1974 and the Fouga Magister from 1978. Over thiry years later these two kits remained the best which were available of these two classic aircraft.

a two-part mould under pressure. When the material cools, the mould is snapped open and the component is ejected ready formed. The principle was developed as early as the 1870s, but remained undeveloped until the 1930s. Development stagnated because of the less-than-perfect characteristics of the early materials, and the low market value of the products for which the

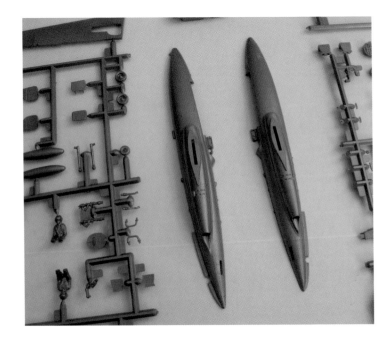

process was typically used. Small and regular-shaped items, such as buttons and collar stays, could cope with the tendency of cellulose acetate to warp as it cooled. Moulding larger and more intricate shaped items such as the Penguin model kits was trickier. Individual mouldings had to be supervised by an experienced mould operator to avoid a high rate of warped components. Increased costs due to wastage was also not helped by the common practice of paying operators on a piece rate basis for their work!

Making the moulds was also a time-consuming and very expensive process. The starting point was usually a drawing – often a set of engineering drawings if the subject was complex. These drawings were in turn used to make an original component or pattern of the intended

The 1:48 scale Airfix Hurricane. The contents of the box in its early 1990s packaging, and a completed kit which had been used as a box top illustration ten years previously. Airfix kits have always had a justified reputation for being well engineered. This enables a kit sometimes to remain in the catalogue literally for decades. Even quite a simple kit such as this Hurricane can be built into a very acceptable replica, especially if care and attention is devoted to painting and decal application.

moulded product. Such patterns were typically fabricated by a craftsman from wood and were often bigger than the intended final part in order to create more detail when the shape was reduced in size. The pattern was then coated in resin which, when dry, formed an exact copy of the shape in a depression in the resin. A layer of wax was then applied to the surface of the depression to represent the thickness of plastic on the finished part. More resin was then applied and when this was removed from the wax, a replica of the two halves of the mould for the one component existed in resin. These shapes were then transferred via a cutter controlled by a pantograph to two steel blocks – the pantograph reproducing the contours of the original and reducing the size. This created the two halves of the mould. Finally the runners – the channels which allowed the molten plastic to flow into the mould – had to be carefully cut in by hand, and the entire inner surface of the mould highly polished.

Designing the mould is therefore a key process, and even a simple plastic construction kit required a very complex mould. The Frog Penguins pushed injection moulding to its limits, and the financial costs of this were reflected in the retail costs of the kits. Prices ranged from 3s for the tiny Percival Gull through to 15s for the Short Singapore flying boat. In order to recoup this

In later years, the Folland Gnat became famous as the first aircraft flown by the RAF Red Arrows display team. In 1964 however, the aircraft was simply the RAF's new advanced trainer, and Airfix obliged with a neat little kit. Undoubtedly many builders aspired to be in the student's seat of the real thing within a few years.

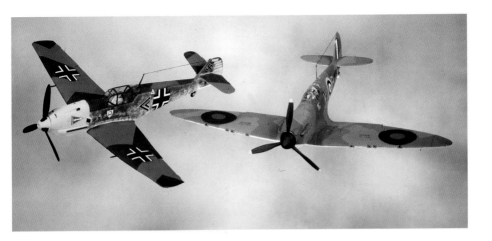

investment, Frog heavily promoted the range – even taking out a full front-page advert in the *Daily Mail* in December 1937.

However, revolutionary as they were, the Penguins were hampered by the unstable nature of cellulose acetate. A better material was needed. Polystyrene had first been identified in the 1830s and was a much more stable material, but it remained of interest only to chemists until the 1930s. It was suitable for injection moulding, but required higher temperatures and pressures and finer tolerance in the moulds themselves. The investment to develop this material could not be supported by model aircraft, but the 1930s provided two other economic drivers. The first was the expansion of domestic electricity supplies and consequently a huge demand for non-conducting fittings. Polystyrene and injection moulding were ideal for this purpose. The second was the rush to rearmament in the 1930s, followed by the Second World War itself. Aircraft in particular demanded large numbers of lightweight fittings of a complex nature, and injection moulding and polystyrene were rapidly developed to meet these needs.

With the end of the Second World War, the wartime manufacturing base was suddenly available to meet a pent-up demand for consumer goods of all types. The war years had been an austere time, and factories with their refined injection moulding techniques were quickly adapted to the manufacture of telephone handsets, hairdryers, vacuum cleaners and the like. The Frog Penguins went back into production, but they were still expensive and with material shortages the kits were not of a consistent quality, undermining their marketability. Polystyrene was the new 'wonder material' and it could be made into anything from cheap toys to combs. As the Airfix company already knew, combs were an ideal product for injection moulding.

The result of two decades of development in plastic model kits. By 1970, Airfix was producing giant 1:24 scale 'super kits'. On the left is the Messerschmitt Bf 109, and on the right the Supermarine Spitfire Mark One.

THE EARLY YEARS – KOVE, COMBS AND KITS

The Ferguson Tractor was sold both as a completed model and, later, as the first Airfix construction kit. Although large numbers of both completed models and kits were produced, surviving examples are very rare.

Airfix was founded by a Jewish Hungarian émigré Nicholas Kove (1891–1958). Kove had an interesting and colourful life: during the First World War he served as a cavalry officer in the Austro-Hungarian Army. Captured and imprisoned in Siberia by the Russians, he escaped and walked back to his home in the Carpathian Mountains, a journey of about 800 miles. After the First World War he became involved in politics, but when the Government in Hungary was overthrown, he moved into business.

The political situation in Europe forced Kove into an itinerant lifestyle. The rise of fascism in Eastern Europe drove him to Barcelona, where he established a plastics factory. When the Spanish Civil War broke out he relocated to Italy, where he was involved in a venture for stiffening shirt collars using a product called 'Interfix'. When the political situation in Italy in turn became difficult, Kove found refuge in England, where he founded Airfix in 1939.

At first the company specialised in making inflatable toys. The name 'Airfix' came about because many of the products the company made were inflatable toys such as swimming rings, and air-filled items such as dolls' heads. Kove apparently had a fondness for names ending in 'ix' and as a non-native English speaker thought the name suggested 'fixed by air'. As it began with an 'A' it also appeared earlier in trade catalogues.

Early Airfix products were predominantly made from rubber, but supplies were seriously disrupted when Japan entered the Second World War. To remain in business Kove began to utilise synthetic materials, but often shortages were such that recycled scrap such as broken fountain pen bodies had to be used. After the war, however, Kove wanted to expand and took the decision to invest in a new injection-moulding machine. Again, the plastic raw material still tended to be scrap, but Kove saw opportunities and used this investment to develop and market cheap mass-produced plastic combs. For a time in the late 1940s Airfix made virtually every comb in the UK.

The breakthrough into plastic kits came about in 1949, when Airfix was commissioned by the Ferguson company to create a model of its latest tractor. The order was significant, with Ferguson wanting 14,400 models to be used as free promotional items. To keep costs down, the model was moulded as separate polystyrene components, but they were assembled in the factory by Airfix. The tractor was very popular, and seeing an opportunity,

The Renault Dauphine was one of a number of everyday motor cars which were released in 1961. Airfix used a smaller scale than many other manufacturers for their car kit – 1:32 – in order for the kits to be competitively priced and fit into the polythene bag packaging.

The Gloster Gladiator was the first biplane kit produced by Airfix in 1956. This is how the kit appeared when it was sold in the mid-1960s. The kit was notable for having the pilot's head moulded in the two fuselage halves, but it was dimensionally an accurate replica – so much so that it was reissued by Airfix in 2008. Kove got his investment back on this mould at least!

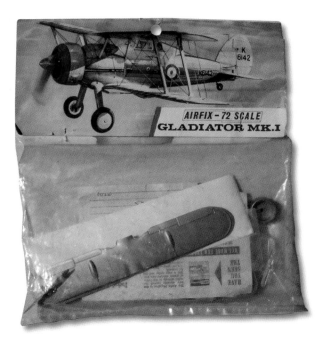

Airfix acquired the rights to market the product as a retail item. This sold well, but being hand-assembled by Airfix it was expensive to produce, and returns of damaged items were high, which affected profitability.

Preferable, it was thought, would be an item like the tractor, but one where the customer did the assembly work. The tractor was accordingly marketed as a kit from 1949. These kits were well presented, with the parts attached to a tray within a box and sold for 8s 6d. This was a high price, when the average wage in Britain at the time was £7 per week. Jim Russon, a buyer for Woolworths (one of Airfix's main retailers), felt instinctively that a lower-priced plastic kit would sell in large numbers, but Kove was reluctant to

The Dennis Fire Engine and 1910 B Type Omnibus: two classic Airfix kits that helped to set the Airfix style, both in terms of subject and box art.

commit the investment necessary. Instead, he wanted to maximise the return from the moulds that had already been made for the tractor.

Meanwhile, American manufacturers were independently developing the concept of the plastic kit. In 1946, a company called Varney produced kits of a submarine and Stearman trainer aircraft in a synthetic material called Tenite. In the same year Hawk released a kit of a Curtis racing biplane moulded in cellulose acetate. In effect, these kits were analogous to the Frog Penguins. However, in 1947 a company called O-Lin – later to become Lindberg – produced a kit of the new P80 jet fighter in polystyrene. Polystyrene soon became the material of choice, with other companies such as Renwall, Gowland & Gowland and Aurora entering the marketplace. They were soon joined by established wooden kit manufacturers such as Strombecker and Monogram who at first added plastic components to their kits, but then moved to the new technology. At first these American kits were expensive and were only sold in specialist hobby stores, but the focus quickly moved to wider sales in department stores at cheaper prices.

Following a fact-finding trip to America, two of Kove's managers, John Gray and Ralph Ehrmann, decided to take up Russon's suggestion and produce plastic construction kits for the British market. However, rather than aircraft, which was the favoured subject matter in America, Airfix chose the *Golden Hind*: a sixteenth-century Elizabethan galleon. To modern eyes this might seem a curious choice, but in 1952 Queen Elizabeth had succeeded to the throne, Germany had recently been defeated, Everest had been conquered and a warship from the reign of the first Queen Elizabeth thus seemed a safe patriotic investment. The *Golden Hind* had also already been released by Gowland & Gowland in America as part of a 'ship in a bottle' kit, and moulds were easy to copy. The only problem was the proposed retail price.

Airfix pitched the new kit to Woolworths at a suggested price of 5s (25p in post-1971 money). Woolworths said that 2s (10p) was the maximum they had in mind. Needing the contract, Gray abandoned the original idea of boxing the kit, and instead proposed marketing the kit in a clear plastic bag with the instructions on the reverse side of a simple paper header stapled to the bag. This form of packaging became an Airfix standard and was used for nearly twenty years – instantly recognisable and irresistibly attractive because of its visible

The imagery of the Second World War was very common in popular culture and especially boys' comics during the 1950s, 1960s and 1970s.

contents. It was a piece of marketing genius, even though the core idea was driven by a tight budget! The *Golden Hind* appeared in 1954, and was an instant success. For months the Airfix factory could not keep up with demand. This kit remained in the Airfix range for over fifty years, but despite its enduring appeal, high levels of sales could not continue indefinitely. A new subject was needed for a follow-up kit. A Spitfire might seem to have been an ideal choice, but Kove did not agree. He believed that the company should continue with more ship models, as the *Golden Hind* was a proven success. Accordingly, more ships followed in 1955, some based on Gowland & Gowland kits, but others (such as the *Cutty Sark*) were Airfix originals. Kove eventually agreed to a Spitfire kit, but remained unconvinced, and threatened to charge the cost of the mould to Gray and Ehrmann if their idea failed to make a profit.

A built example of the BTK Spitfire. Not a terribly accurate kit, but good enough for the early 1950s.

The details of this Spitfire reveal that one of the fact-finding trips to America may have yielded more than inspiration: Aurora's 1954 Spitfire kit was effectively identical to the Airfix kit. The Airfix kit was smaller, in 1:72 rather than 1:48 scale – to fit within the 2s price bracket stipulated by Woolworths – but the dimensional inaccuracies of the Aurora original were replicated. The two kits had the same breakdown and number of parts, and even the decal sheet portrayed an aircraft with the same incorrect squadron markings – 'BTK'. Records have been lost as to whether or not Airfix obtained a licence to copy either the Gowland & Gowland or Aurora kits, but the design of kits was in its infancy, and copying existing moulds was common practice.

The original 1:72 scale Airfix Spitfire 'BTK'. Surviving unmade examples are rare and the packaging is often a little battered.

Despite its inaccuracies, the Spitfire that went on sale in 1955 was an instant success. A reason for this could have been that the item tapped into the huge interest in the Second World War, which was beginning to be reflected in popular culture in 1950s Britain. Films such as *Reach for the Sky*, *Angels One Five* and *The Dambusters* (all of which appeared early in the decade) helped to define how the war was visualised by later generations. Themes and images of the Second World War were also common in books and children's comics from this period until the early 1980s. The artwork in these comics was vivid and technically accurate, and the appearance of the inexpensive plastic kit created the ideal outlet for boys – and it was mainly boys and their fathers – to recast their imagination into a solid form. Almost by chance Airfix found itself in the right place at the right time to capitalise on these underlying trends. The company was quickly able to move forward into a period of profitability and expansion which was to be the envy of its rivals.

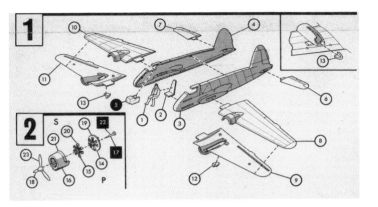

Airfix instruction sheet from the 1960s.

The number of new kits produced was extraordinarily and consistently high, year after year. Twenty new kits were produced in 1957, rising in 1958 and 1959 to twenty-four new kits a year. This pattern continued until the early 1970s, with twenty-five new kits in 1972 and eighteen in 1973. This output reflected the fact that Airfix had a hugely successful product that sold in sufficient numbers for constant innovation to be necessary. The choice of subjects is also revealing: following the success of the BTK Spitfire, aircraft designed by Airfix began to dominate the release schedule. The first of these was the Gloster Gladiator biplane fighter, which appeared in 1956. In the same year the Messerschmitt Bf 109 was the first 'opposition' Second World War aircraft, and the Westland Whirlwind was the first helicopter. In 1957 no fewer than eleven aircraft ranging from the tiny First World War Fokker Dr1 triplane (of *Red Baron* fame) to the first two larger aircraft attempted by Airfix – the Spitfire's ugly sister, the Supermarine Walrus amphibian, and the de Havilland Mosquito. The following year saw the first American aircraft – a P51 Mustang – and the Mig 15 was both the first jet and first Soviet subject tackled by Airfix.

Such subjects were popular and profitable, and the subjects to some extent chose themselves, but Airfix also made some eccentric choices for kits, such as the Saunders Roe SR53 rocket aircraft and Grumman Gosling (1958), and the Fairey Rotodyne experimental gyroplane a year later. The same eccentricity is apparent in the Edwardian B Type Omnibus (from 1962) and the Dennis Fire Engine (from 1964): both are classic Airfix kits and are brilliant modelling subjects, but no one knew what they were missing until they arrived. It was such innovation that helped to propel and sustain Airfix through what was its first 'golden age'.

The untroubled days of motoring in the 1970s: simpler times, a little machismo and not a care for the environment. This was every thirteen-year-old boy's dream – the car as well as the girl!

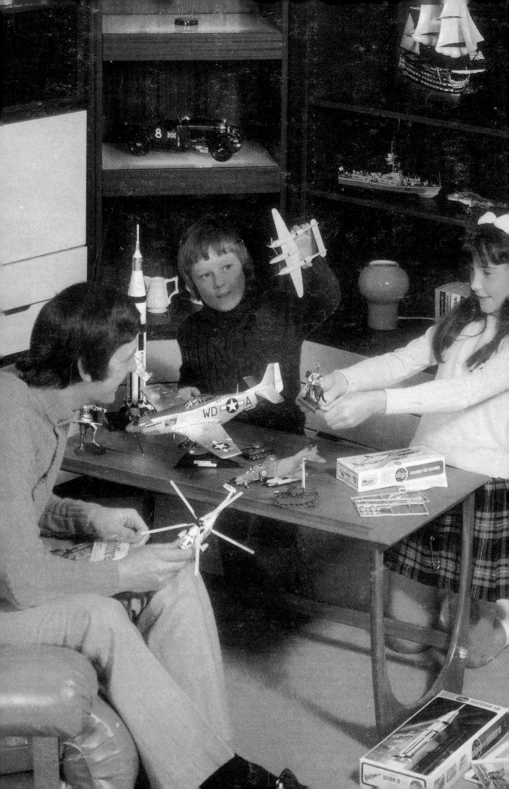

THE GOLDEN YEARS

N ICHOLAS KOVE died in 1958 and Gray and Ehrmann took over. Ehrmann focused on general management and marketing, while Gray concentrated on kit selection and design. Under the direction of these two managers, the brand moved forward confidently into the next two decades. Other competing kit manufacturers emerged in the same period, but Airfix was always the market leader in Britain and the Commonwealth, and had few rivals on the world stage.

The company's prolific output rapidly built up a back catalogue that soon became the envy of many competitors. This catalogue was doubly effective because almost from the start of kit production, Airfix had adopted the concept of 'constant scale'. Other manufactures, especially American ones, tended to scale their kits to fit a commonly sized box. This often resulted in aircraft, for example, being variously 1:54, 1:65, 1:79, 1:121, 1:139, or whatever scale made the best use of the available box. The finished models were all approximately the same size, but could look very odd when displayed together.

The early Airfix ships had adopted this variable approach to scale, to enable them to fit into the standard 2s Woolworth bags; but other subjects were produced to a constant scale so that cars, figures or aircraft could be displayed realistically together. This appealed to children, who often wanted to stage a mock dog fight with their models, as well as to serious modellers who were more interested in building a themed collection that could be displayed together.

The scale chosen for most aircraft was 1:72, the scale used for the pre-war Skybird solid kits and the Penguin. This scale results in quite a small model for a Second World War fighter, which was a typical early Airfix subject. There was the added advantage that a Spitfire, a Hurricane or a Messerschmitt Bf 109 fitted perfectly into a 2s plastic bag.

The bigger, more elaborate kits tended to be for birthdays and Christmas, whereas the polythene bag kits were squarely aimed at weekend pocket-money buys. These kits sold in enormous numbers and easily justified the

Opposite:
Cover image
from the Airfix
catalogue of 1973.
Airfix modelling
was portrayed as
an activity for the
whole family.

In the 1960s new technology was often portrayed in an exciting and optimistic manner. Airfix tapped into this mood perfectly.

investment in their moulds. Another factor favouring the smaller model was the physical capacity of the injection-moulding machines used by Airfix in the initial phase of kit production. For some years, these machines were capable of producing only small mouldings. Accordingly, when Airfix began to tackle larger subjects, they had to design the kits carefully to make the best use of the size of components their machines could produce. This limitation was the reason why, when Airfix started to model larger aircraft such as airliners, they had to introduce a new constant scale of 1:144. Eventually, Airfix acquired machines to make larger components, but 1:144 scale remained a popular legacy.

A 1960s catalogue shot of the 1:32 scale series of cars: family runabouts to sports cars.

Larger kits required a more robust form of packaging than the simple 2s plastic bags. Twin-engined Second World War aircraft, such as the Lockheed P38 from 1938, initially appeared in plastic bags, but were soon sold in boxes. This development was mainly to protect the components, but substantial packaging also conferred a sense of added value. With the contents out of view, Airfix created the idea of sequencing the kits into 'series'. The series system cut across subjects, and was intended to categorise the kits in terms of price, size and complexity. A Series 1 kit, for example, was anything that fitted into the plastic bag packaging, and was – by virtue of its size – likely to be a relatively simple kit to build. Series 2 was one step further on, and would typically be a twin-engined Second World War aircraft. A Series 3 kit would be a small Second World War bomber, and so on. This system has been retained, and variations on the theme are still a feature of several of Airfix's rivals.

Aircraft were and still are the core of the Airfix catalogue, but a large proportion of the early kits were buildings and trackside accessories for model railway builders. The importance of this side of Airfix is often overlooked in any history of the brand, but a significant number of the earlier kits were aimed at railway modellers, with Airfix quite consciously building up this side of their range quickly once the potential of plastic kits was apparent. So important was railway modelling that in 1962, Airfix acquired the 'Kitmaster' line produced by the British doll company Rosebud to strengthen this side of their business. Many of these kits and the early Airfix-originated railway accessories are still available and continue to be used by railway modellers the world over.

Ironically, for a company that pioneered the concept of 'constant scale', the exact scale of the Airfix railway accessories has been a little ambivalent at times. Early model railway sets and layouts tended to have variable scales, but commonality was eventually standardised by the need of manufacturers to have as wide a market as possible for their accessories. In Europe the two dominant scales by the mid-1950s were OO and HO. The predominately British OO equated

Everyday motoring when the motorways were jam-free. Unfortunately, most trips to the seaside were in Dad's sensible Herald, not a Beach Buggy.

A frontispiece from a 1970s catalogue displays the diverse Airfix range.

In 1969 the first
generation of
Harrier 'Jump Jets'
entered RAF
service and won
a London to New
York air race.
Airfix reflected
both events with
the first plastic kit
of the aircraft in
1:72 scale.
Harriers rarely
took off vertically,
but Roy Cross, one
of Airfix's most
talented artists,
used a little
artistic licence
to great effect.

A 1960s catalogue
shot of some of
the rolling stock
range.
Stephenson's
Rocket was
a particularly
popular kit.

to 1:76 scale, and HO (the favoured scale in the rest of Europe) equated to 1:87. Airfix originally designed and marketed their trackside accessories at OO scale. However, to broaden their appeal, they were soon badged as being of OO/HO scale – that is to say, compatible with both scales. Despite the fact that 1:87 is significantly smaller than 1:76, Airfix persisted with the view that they were interchangeable for some time.

Confusion over scales also affected the very successful figure range. Airfix produced a range of platform figures in 1958, and quickly followed these with sets of farm animals, zoo animals and general street scene figures. Again, these figures were originally OO but were quickly marketed as OO/HO even though they were actually too large to look realistic in the smaller scale. Nevertheless, the figures were hugely successful and led to Airfix introducing a range of figure sets. These sets were moulded in flexible polythene rather than the harder polystyrene used for kits, and were aimed at both serious war gamers as well as the inexpensive toy market. The range of figures produced was comprehensive: soldiers from various ages were predominant, but cowboys, Indians, Romans, Ancient Britons and even astronauts were included.

1, 2, 4 AND 5
OO/HO ROLLING STOCK

01661-2 Stephenson's Rocket. The most famous early British locomotive, the Rocket is reproduced with rotating wheels and working connecting rods, a tender and two finely sculptured figures in period costume.

SERIES 2

02656-3 Esso Tank Wagon. This Airfix Tank Wagon Kit contains 46 parts. Modelled on the Esso Class 'B' type suitable for carrying up to 35 tons of fuel oil, diesel oil or kerosene.

02657-6 B.R. 16-Ton Mineral Wagon. This 16-ton Mineral Wagon has operating doors for loose loads plus fixed dummy load.

02658-9 Brake Van. Moulded in B.R. matt brown, this 46-part kit contains choice of couplings, brake lamps, running boards, vacuum pipes, brake shoes, and vacuum brake cylinder. Transfer sheet provides correct markings to complete this essential piece of equipment.

02659-2 B.R. Cattle Wagon. This 40-part kit is modelled on the standard B.R. Cattle Wagon. Real loading and unloading operations can be carried out because the doors actually work.

02660-2 0-4-0 Saddle Tank Locomotive. This tiny locomotive was designed for use in the restricted space of shunting yards and docks. The kit has a wealth of detail and operating features.

SERIES 4

04452-7 Schools Class 'Harrow'. The famous 'Schools' class were the heaviest 4-4-0 type locomotives in Britain. They were introduced in 1930 and operated by the Southern Railway.

04653-0 B.R. Mogul. The 2-6-0 'Moguls' which were introduced in 1952 were among the last steam locomotives to be operated by British Railways. 115 were built and used on all except the Western Region.

SERIES 5

05651-7 Battle of Britain Class 'Eiggin Hill'. Built in 1946 for express passenger services, the 'Battle of Britain' class is easily recognized by the streamlined casing. Most of the class were named after RAF squadrons or airfields.

05652-0 'Evening Star'. The last steam locomotive to be built for British Railways, the 'Evening Star' was named at Swindon in March 1960. Every detail of the powerful 2-10-0 original is captured in this fully-detailed kit.

Railway items were always a very popular element of the Airfix range.

The extensive range of OO/HO figures took a final small step with this set of astronaut figures.

To the millions of children who must have painted and played with these figures, the details may not have mattered as they did to purists. These sets have retained their popularity into the twenty-first century – possibly because the detailed but tiny individual figures were sucked up by vacuum cleaners as quickly as new ones were moulded!

Moving up in scale a little, 1959 saw the first five kits in a range of 1:12 figures. These kits were mainly of historical or typically British figures: Napoleon, the Black Prince and a Coldstream Guardsman were among the first kits to appear, and they were a conscious effort on the part of Airfix to broaden the appeal and market of their products. The figure kits were vaguely educational in nature, and tended to be bought as presents by adults who slightly disapproved of the subject matter of the Airfix kit their nephew really wanted. However, to the average young builder, any Airfix kit was better than none.

The final significant addition to the range of figures were the tiny but highly detailed kits in the traditional toy soldier scale of '54 mm' – the height of a 5 foot 8 inch person in 1:32 scale. Very specialist and expensive kits in this scale had been available since the mid-1960s from a French company called Historex. In 1971, Airfix decided to compete and began a Collectors Series of mainly Napoleonic figures. These were very affordable, being in Series 1 for standing figures and Series 2 for mounted ones. The kits provided a useful source of spare parts for adult modellers, as well as an immense amount of frustration for the less experienced who were tempted by the subject matter.

Given their specialist nature, Airfix could have marketed these kits at a considerably higher retail price than they did, but there was always a sense of inclusiveness about Airfix. A tiny kit was a tiny kit, and even if it was aimed at adults who were used to paying more, it was in Series 1 for small-change prices.

The 54 mm kits were evidence of a trend that had begun as soon as the very first kits were designed. As well as expanding in numbers, the individual kits also rapidly evolved in complexity. This was partly due to a greater maturity and confidence in the mould-making process, but also due to competition between manufacturers

Above:
The hovercraft prototype – cutting-edge British technology from the 1960s – both the full-sized vehicle and the model.

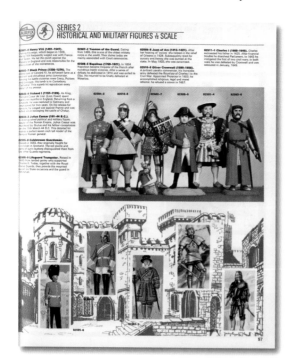

Left: The historical figure range: Julius Caesar, Oliver Cromwell, the Black Prince, Napoleon, Henry VIII and Richard I.

and increasing expectation from customers. The very early aircraft kits such as the Gloster Gladiator from 1956 simply had a pilot's head and shoulders moulded into the fuselage halves under a clear canopy. Within a couple of years, the cockpits were open and provided with a pilot figure. Soon the pilot figure got a seat and by the mid-1960s – especially in the larger kits – cockpits started to acquire floors, control sticks and instrument panels. Internal detail also began to appear inside undercarriage bays and behind jet intakes. Since the 1980s, most kits have been comprehensively detailed in

Chieftain and Leopard tanks were standard NATO equipment in the late 1960s. Airfix reflected the current Cold War as well as historic vehicles.

The Coldstream Guards, which appeared in 1959, were Airfix's first non-railway orientated OO/HO figures.

Airfix linked up with Quantas Airways to produce a special edition of the Avro 504K for the Australian airline to use as a promotional item in the 1960s. Such special edition kits are now highly collectable.

these areas, and standards have continued to rise, but it is fair to say that Airfix kits led the way with their close attention to detail.

Surprisingly, the first Airfix catalogue did not appear until 1962, but the publication of the annual catalogue soon became an eagerly awaited event. Looking back at the contents of the early catalogues, it is clear that Airfix was providing both the material to reflect on a recently won victory in the Second World War, but also a mirror to what Prime Minister Harold Wilson referred to as a period of 'white hot technical revolution'. The push given to technology in the Second World War had continued into the Cold War, and Airfix answered this with kits of supersonic aircraft, moon rockets, giant hovercraft, sports cars, missile-armed destroyers and huge ocean-going liners. If something had wings, wheels, tracks or a propeller, Airfix either had a kit of it or had one planned. The output of new kits was phenomenal, and for most of the 1960s and early 1970s, many schoolboys (and some schoolgirls) made Airfix kits on a regular basis.

During the 1950s, 1960s and 1970s some domestic competition for Airfix appeared in the form first of Frog and later Lesney. After the Second World War, International Model Aircraft concentrated on producing Frog ready-made flying model aircraft, but in 1955, encouraged by the early success of Airfix, another Lines Brothers subsidiary, Rovex, began using the name 'Frog' for a new range of polystyrene-based kits.

To avoid direct competition with Airfix, Rovex tended to choose slightly more esoteric subjects for their Frog kits. They were also never as prolific and

For a time in the 1960s it seemed as though the hovercraft would be the future of transport.

tended to bulk up the size of their catalogue by producing kits under licence from other manufacturers such as Renwall from America and Hasegawa from Japan. Frog also never had the retail outlet volume afforded to Airfix via the link with Woolworths, and their kits tended to be more expensive and aimed more at serious modellers than the general market. As a consequence, Frog obtained a large market niche, but they were never serious rivals to a dominant Airfix.

Lesney and their Matchbox brand offered sterner competition. Matchbox was perhaps the world's most famous name associated with die-cast models, and it was something of a shock when, in 1972, the brand was used for a new range of plastic kits. Unlike Frog, Lesney invested heavily in new tooling, and already had a recognised brand name with strong trade distribution. As a consequence, during the 1970s and 1980s the new kits gave Airfix some serious competition. Matchbox kits were aggressively priced and were of a consistent standard. (By the 1970s some of the Airfix moulds were twenty years old and the quality could vary considerably.) Matchbox also moulded their kits in two or more colours, covered areas such as Formula One, which had been ignored by Airfix, and included innovations

Two New Waterline Models
67 parts make up the highly detailed waterline model of HMS Hood, the largest British battlecruiser of the Second World War until she was sunk in the Second World War. The Bismarck, one of the German fleet's most powerful and heavily armed battleships was sunk in perhaps the most famous naval encounter of the War. The kit has 49 high definition parts. These two clip-together kits are in 1/1200th scale.

SA 341 Gazelle
The SA 341 Gazelle is a streamlined 2-seater military helicopter with the unusual feature of a tail rotor built into the tail fin. The 1/72nd scale kit has more than 40 parts and includes transfers for Army markings.

The June 1974 edition of the *Airfix Magazine* carried a typical advertisement for three new kits issued that month. Colour was limited to the front cover of the magazine for virtually its entire history.

The Series 1 HMS *Victory* dated from 1956. It remained a popular kit for some years and by the late 1980s, following polythene bags and blister packs, was packaged in a small box.

The Matchbox kits represented serious competition for a time. The two-colour presentation of the kits was highly innovative.

such as diorama bases in their tank and armoured vehicle kits. Serious modellers thought that the differently coloured sprues were a gimmick, but they were there to attract younger builders, and they were effective in that aim.

Matchbox eventually grew to become a serious rival to Airfix, but there was realistically no prospect of another company supplanting Airfix until the 1980s. Airfix had a better system of distribution, and a brand name that had already become the generic term for the products of its competitors. Airfix was even confident enough to have its own monthly magazine, launched in June 1960. At first it was a showcase for Airfix products, but it quickly became an editorially independent magazine for the wider modelling community. The magazine carried a range of features on building, improving and converting kits, together with articles on war gaming and history, so that modellers could understand fully the context of their models. The magazine also carried impartial reviews of other manufacturers' kits – giving credit where credit was due – and illustrating the confidence Airfix had in its own products.

In the 1970s the magazine led to a series of generic modelling guides, and a yearly annual. The 1970s also saw the appearance of a series of titles focusing on a single aircraft, ship or tank. Each subject was related to a specific kit, with the book intended to be both a history and a guide to get the best from the kit. This type of 'affinity' publishing was still successfully pursued decades later by manufacturers such as Games Workshop and Tamiya.

In the 1960s and 1970s Airfix moved into the realm of acquiring licences to produce kits associated with popular films and television programmes. Notable kits included figures of James Bond and Odd Job from *Goldfinger* and the 'Little Nellie' autogyro from *You Only Live Twice*. The Pan Am Orion spacecraft from *2001: A Space Odyssey* was also a very popular kit in the late 1960s, as was a set of figures linked to *The High Chaparral* television series. There was also a set of figures of Robin Hood and his company. (Although the box art for this set was clearly inspired by Errol Flynn, no mention was made of the classic Hollywood film produced a couple of decades previously – lawyers would be more on-the-ball in the twenty-first century!)

Airfix had a productive association with Gerry and Sylvia Anderson, although surprisingly they never produced a kit from the Andersons' most famous television series, *Thunderbirds*. The year 1968 did, however, see the Angel Interceptor aircraft from *Captain Scarlet* appear, and in 1976 the Eagle transporter spacecraft from *Space 1999* was created. Intriguingly, Airfix also had a link with the Andersons via two 'lost kits' featuring the starring vehicles from *Fireball XL5* and *Stingray* – the two puppet series that immediately pre-dated *Thunderbirds* and *Captain Scarlet*. The moulds for both kits were made by Airfix, but they were produced in plain boxes as a promotion by the Lyons Maid ice cream company. The 'Zoom' ice lolly was marketed at boys, being shaped like a rocket, with a picture card in its wrapper and often featuring a promotional offer. Two offers in 1963 and 1964 were for kits of *Fireball XL5* and *Stingray* for the princely sum of two Zoom wrappers and 4s 6d. Both kits are now incredibly rare and are highly valued amongst collectors. The Lyons Maid

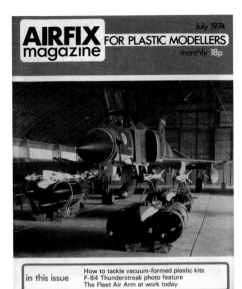

The cover of the July 1974 edition of the *Airfix Magazine*. Now a museum piece, the RAF Phantom was, at the time, the final word in fighter design.

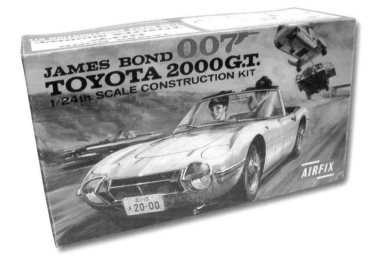

The 1960s saw several kits inspired by James Bond, all of which became very collectable in later years.

lollipop aimed at girls was called 'FAB' and used Lady Penelope from *Thunderbirds* in its advertising, but in 1965 girls were not thought of as being great kit builders and there was no kit of Lady Penelope's pink Rolls-Royce!

Definitely not pink or in plain boxes were two kits that epitomised Airfix in this period – the 1:24 Spitfire and the 1:12 'Blower' Bentley car. These two quintessentially British subjects were simply stunning in terms of design and complexity when they appeared as 'Superkits' in 1970 and 1971. The American company Revell had been producing 1:32 scale aircraft kits since the late 1960s. These were large kits by the standards of the day, but the decision by Airfix to go to 1:24 scale for an aircraft and 1:12 for a vintage car was a bold statement for the company to make. The Spitfire had a fully equipped interior including a Merlin engine, which was more detailed in its own right than

The Angel Interceptor aircraft from the Gerry Anderson series *Captain Scarlet* was a very popular kit.

A 1960s catalogue showing a range of 1:72 scale aircraft.

A photograph from a 1970s catalogue of the remarkable 1:12 scale Bentley Le Mans car, the only large-scale car produced by Airfix.

many smaller kits. The 1:12 Bentley was a response to the similar scale Formula 1 and sports cars being produced by the Japanese company Tamiya, but as with the Spitfire, the Bentley raised the bar by feet, not inches. A large-scale car can have more visible internal detail than an aircraft, so Airfix adopted the approach of taking a surviving Bentley, and making a scaled copy of literally every component.

Left: Catalogue illustration shot of some Series 3 aircraft range from the same period. Unlike their Series 1 cousins, these required a couple of weeks' pocket money or a birthday postal order from an uncle!

Below: *Star Wars* kits were popular in the late 1970s. Many kits were originated by AMT in America and reissued by Airfix.

SOMETHING FOR
EVERYONE: THE 1970s

B Y THE MID-1970s Airfix was in an enviable position. Kits were being sold as quickly as the moulding machines could turn them out, and new kits appeared at a rate that challenged even the most committed enthusiasts' building speed. In common with most manufacturers, aircraft formed the core of the range, but there was literally something to suit everyone's taste.

THE KITS

ROCKETS AND SPACESHIPS
Between 1968 and 1978, during the Space Race, a small range of classic kits was produced in 1:72 and 1:144 scale. A larger-scale kit of the Lunar Rover from the later Apollo missions unfortunately remained on the drawing board.

Opposite: A small series of 1:8 scale motorbikes made challenging but highly detailed models.

Left: The Russian space programme was also covered by Airfix.

MOTORCYCLES

A difficult subject matter for inexperienced modellers, but some moulds inherited from Kitmaster and a small home-grown range included an Ariel, a BSA, a Honda and a BMW, all of which were beautiful models. Some interesting contemporary models originating from Heller moulds were added in the 1990s.

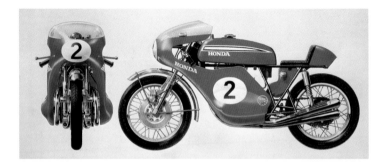

Top: Airfix often challenged consumers to 'spot the difference' in their publicity material. This kit of a Honda racing bike shows exactly why.

Middle and bottom: The Arial Arrow kit was acquired from Kitmaster when Airfix purchased their moulds.

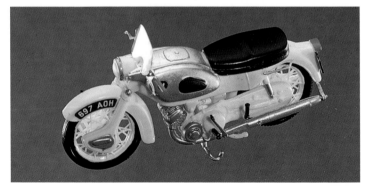

Part of the warship range from the early 1970s.

WARSHIPS

Starting in 1959 with the aircraft carrier HMS *Victorious*, Airfix focused on the Second World War and contemporary Royal Navy subjects in 1:600 scale. Classic 'enemy' vessels such as the *Tirpitz* and *Scharnhorst* also enabled mock naval engagements as well as dog fights to be fought. Highly detailed kits in 1:72 scale of smaller Second World War vessels such as the Vosper Motor Torpedo Boats, the RAF Rescue Launch and the German 'E' Boat were also very popular kits.

The small classic ships range.

Model T Ford kit had originally appeared in the polythene bag packaging, but by the late 1970s it was in a small box complete with suitably impressive box art.

CLASSIC HISTORICAL SHIPS

Surprisingly, this area is one in which Airfix did not adopt a 'constant scale', but rather designed both the smaller *Golden Hind* series and the latter larger models to fit the available packaging. This was a pragmatic approach given the relative sizes of some the original subjects.

CARS

Many car kits that have appeared in Airfix boxes have been reboxing of other manufacturers' kits – particularly MPC, Aoshima and Heller – since the 1980s. At the height of their power in the 1970s, however, Airfix could boast the outstanding 1:12 Bentley, and a nice range of vintage to contemporary

A superbly constructed example of the Beam Engine kit. This kit, if carefully built, could be made up into a working motorised model.

The Airfix dinosaurs were fun and colourful, but they would have benefited from modern palaeontological research!

cars in 1:32. Complementing this series were the two outstanding kits mentioned previously: the 1914 Dennis Fire Engine and the B Type Omnibus, which could be built in civilian guise or as a First World War troop carrier.

COLLECTORS' SERIES

Trevithick's steam railway locomotive of 1804, a beam engine, Maudslay's 1827 marine engine and a cutaway four-stroke internal combustion engine were available in kit form to demonstrate the basic principles of engineering. All of these could be motorised.

DINOSAURS

Dinosaurs were popular even before *Jurassic Park*, and Airfix was one of a number of manufacturers who produced a range of models. They were great fun, especially to the modern eye, in that they illustrate the limited knowledge of dinosaur anatomy in the 1970s!

TRAINS AND TRACKSIDE ACCESSORIES

Despite the confusion of scales, the contribution by Airfix to many enthusiasts' railway dioramas is undeniable.

MILITARY VEHICLES

The Second World War formed the core of an extensive range in 1:76 scale, which included airfield vehicles and landing craft. The SAM 2 missile from the Vietnam and Middle East conflicts was an outstanding kit in this range, as was a larger 1:32 scale version of Field Marshall Montgomery's staff car.

Despite the passing resemblance to Princess Anne, this show jumper figure did not receive a 'By Royal Appointment' label.

SHOWJUMPER

1/12 SCALE PLASTIC CONSTRUCTION KIT

FIGURES

Setting aside the scale confusion, the 1:76 scale figures were not kits as such, but are still Airfix classics. Figures in 1:32 were added in the 1970s together with a 'multi-pose' range, which enabled the modeller to create a unique figure from sets of generic parts. The 54 mm range were highly detailed kits for the dedicated modeller, whereas the 1:12 range were more general in appeal. The notable kit in this range was a show jumper with a likeness to Princess Anne, who competed for Great Britain in the 1976 Olympic Games.

The Wildlife Series was years ahead of its time in terms of ecological awareness.

WILDLIFE SERIES

Years before making space for wildlife in our gardens was second nature, Airfix saw the potential in marketing a range of wildlife-based kits and produced a small series of British birds to a 1:1 scale.

AIRCRAFT

By the late 1970s Airfix had an extensive and unrivalled range of civilian and military aircraft in 1:72 scale. They had also established the airliner scale of 1:114 and had produced six kits in what was an astonishing 1:24 scale series.

Series 5 kits from the early 1970s.

A STEP TOO FAR?

The 1:24 scale aircraft kits and the 1:12 scale Bentley were the flagship kits of Airfix in the 1970s. The visual impact of such large models is impressive, and they illustrated just how far Airfix had come since the 10p polythene bag kits in Woolworths. The kits were and are stunning, but they were not impulse pocket money purchases by any means. The original retail price of the 1:24 scale Spitfire was twenty-five times the cost of the Series 1 kits then on sale, and it needed a considerable amount of time and patience to complete. For such kits to make economic sense, Airfix had to be confident that they would remain on the birthday- and Christmas-present list for some years, and that enough modellers would continue to have the dedication to build them.

Concerns were raised that Airfix had overstretched themselves, but the Spitfire was a huge success, and was followed by the Messerschmitt Bf 109, the P51 Mustang, the Hurricane, an early Harrier jump jet, the Ju87 Stuka and the Fw190. All of these kits sold well, but the Bentley struggled a little, and no further large-scale cars were attempted. Twenty years previously Kove had been cautious about investment in new moulds. By 1976 the cockpit in the Hurricane made it a far more complex kit than the *Golden Hind* had been. In the twenty-first century, updated versions of these kits still sell well, proving the concept of the vision, but in the late 1970s, sales started to slow badly. Kits of the Gladiator and Mosquito in 1:24 scale were abandoned at design stage; suddenly much more difficult times were upon Airfix.

A wide range of Airfix kits was illustrated on the cover of the 1978 catalogue.

Box art of the first issue of the 1:24 scale Harrier.

SERIES 2

Even better-than-ever value for money
series presents two famous World War
opponents in one box. A unique two-i
display stand enables the finished mod
mounted in realistic air-to-air combat p

02140–3 Camel & Albatros. This do
kit contains 94 parts, a twin instruction
and two sets of transfers to allow the r
to build two of the First World War's m
famous fighters. Both aircraft were sele
the mounts of some of the greatest Ace
Western Front and appeared in a wide
of markings to offer the enthusiast a ra
colourful paint schemes.

**02141–6 Bristol Fighter & Fokker
Triplane.** The diminutive single-seat F
Dr. 1 offers a fascinating contrast to its
adversary in this double kit – the big tv
Bristol F2B. The F2B has a flexible rear
and gunner in the second cockpit, ofte
decisive factor in combat. By the end o
War the Fokker Triplane was obsolete b
Bristol Fighter continued to serve the R
for many years.

02142–9 Roland C-11 & R.E.8. This
brings together two of the best known
World War I observation aircraft and th
completed models are ideally contraste
British R.E.8. more often known as the
Tate' is angular and provided with a mu
of struts and bracing but the German 'V
has a fully streamlined shape years ahe
time. Complete with finely sculptured d
armament.

SERIES 3

Following the success of the World Wa
Dogfight Doubles, we introduce a new
Here again the completed models can b
excitingly displayed on the large two-in
base. Each kit contains one aircraft fron
One and one from Series Two or Three

**03140–6 Beaufighter & Messerschr
Me 109.** This double kit combines the
torpedo carrying Bristol Beaufighter an
late production G-6 version of the Me 1
These war planes were widely used dur
European campaign and often joined ba
during the shipping strikes at low level.
which were the speciality of the Beaufit

**03141–9 Messerschmitt Me 110 &
Spitfire IX.** Brought together here are
the outstanding fighters of World War I
immortal British Spitfire and the Me 110
successful of the sub-types of this twin
fighter. Both of these aircraft were con
developed throughout the war years an
among the few types in action when th
broke out and still operational in 1945.

**03142–2 Mosquito & Messerschm
Me 262.** These two twin-engined figh
piston engined Mosquito and the jet po
Me 262, were among the fastest of all '
War II aircraft. The Mosquito appeared
the war and played a vital role in defea
Luftwaffe, but development of the Me
delayed, largely by the personal interve
Hitler, and when it finally reached large
service it was already too late to influe
course of hostilities.

03143–5 Mirage III & MiG-15. Two
most recently to have seen combat; in
Israeli-Arab conflict of 1967. Both airc
authentic markings.

03144–8 Stormovik & Fw190. The
Russian Stormovik and the German Fw
were both used in the low-level role, th
Stormovik attacking with rocket bombs
Fw 190 with its bomb and heavy canno
contrast between the ungainly Stormov
the sleek Focke-Wulf is well illustrated

03145–1 Cessna O-2 and MiG-21. T
unusual kit brings together two interest
aircraft. The Cessna O–2 push-pull airc
used by the USAF for reconnaissance o
forward positions and the MiG–21 is a
line defence aircraft with many Eastern
countries.

DIFFICULT YEARS
AND A RENAISSANCE

BRITAIN CAME out of the 1970s facing a severe economic recession, rampant inflation, high oil prices and widespread industrial unrest. A Conservative Government led by Margaret Thatcher was ideologically more concerned with free markets and union reform than assisting manufacturing industry. With respect to Airfix, the kit side of the business was still sound, but the company had diversified in the 1970s and acquired a number of other toy brands and their associated factories.

Meccano, the iconic engineering construction system, had been acquired by Airfix in 1972. Like Airfix, Meccano was a British institution, but unlike Airfix, Meccano had industrial relations problems, and very high production costs due to an inefficient factory in Liverpool. The Liverpool workforce refused to accept any job losses or changes to working practices. Strikes were also threatened, and dealing with these problems took time and money, which Airfix did not have. Airfix was forced to declare bankruptcy in 1981, which immediately sealed the fate of the Meccano factory.

The Airfix model business was quickly bought by an American conglomerate, General Mills. General Mills was a food company that had diversified into toy production, via the model company MPC in America and Palitoy in Britain. Palitoy were makers of the hugely successful Action Man figure, and were chosen by General Mills to manage Airfix. The immediate effect on Airfix was the ending of production in Britain and a hiatus in the production of new kits. Palitoy had a factory in France, and all the Airfix moulds were moved there. New kit design was undertaken by Palitoy, and General Mills stipulated that any new tooling had to make a return on its investment within three years. A planned kit of Captain Nemo's submarine from *20,000 Leagues Under the Sea* was cancelled despite the mould having been made, and the majority of new kits that appeared were of American 'muscle cars' and *Star Wars* items designed by MPC. These MPC kits were good, but they were not typical Airfix fare, and the brand soon became a pale reflection of its former self.

Opposite:
How every well-dressed twelve-year-old in the 1970s probably played with their 'Dogfight Doubles' kits!

Palitoy box art for
the vintage Mig 15

At least the Airfix brand survived, unlike its two domestic rivals Frog
and Matchbox. Frog ceased production in 1978 and most of the moulds were
sold to the Soviet Union. Virtually all the kits quickly reappeared under the
Novo label in minimalist packaging. The Novo brand itself is a now a 'retro
classic' for collectors. Novo itself disappeared with the Soviet Union, but

Box art for the
1:48 scale
Lightning kit from
the 1990s.

model making has remained popular in Eastern Europe. Kit brands have
proliferated, and the packaging has become slicker, but the contents are often
still the old Frog kits. The parent company of Matchbox — Lesney —

responded to the difficult 1980s by refocusing on its core die-cast market. The moulds and the right to use the Matchbox label on plastic were sold to the German division of Revell. The Matchbox label continued for a while, but eventually the kits were simply reissued in Revell boxes. It is pleasing that good kits survive and continue to be available for new generations of modellers, but the loss of a brand and the direct heritage that goes with it is nevertheless regrettable.

Airfix, however, was a survivor. General Mills itself withdrew from the toy market in 1985. Revell was interested in acquiring the Airfix brand, but lost out to a chemical company called Borden. This company had a hobby division, which owned the famous modelling paint brand Humbrol and the French kit manufacturer Heller. The Airfix moulds remained in France, but were relocated to the Heller factory in Trun. Potentially, the Humbrol/Heller link was a strong package, but the 1980s saw the arrival of home computing and videos, and the high points of the 1970s for modelling were hard to recapture. Investment was low, and relatively few new kits appeared. During the late 1980s and early 1990s, the shortfall was made up by Heller and other manufacturers' kits appearing in Airfix boxes. This created the appearance of a healthy new release programme, but comparatively little of it was uniquely Airfix.

This situation changed a little in the late 1990s and the early years of the new century. Some investment was made in new models, and Airfix produced a number of superb new kits of some iconic British aircraft. Subjects included 1:48 scale kits of the Lightning jet fighter, a late mark Spitfire and the British Aerospace Hawk trainer in obligatory Red Arrows markings. In 1:72 scale a very nice kit of the TSR2, a cancelled 1960s supersonic bomber, was a notable release, and a very successful association was made with the Wallace and Gromit animated film franchise – continuing the tradition of film- and television-related kits.

Airfix were quick off the mark to produce a kit of the RAF's Hawk trainer when it flew as a prototype in 1974. By the 1980s the aircraft was used by the Red Arrows display team, and Airfix reissued the kit with appropriate markings. So popular was this subject and kit that in 2009, Airfix/Hornby produced two completely new kits of the Hawk to twenty-first century standards – one of a standard Hawk in Red Arrow markings, the other of a later generation aircraft.

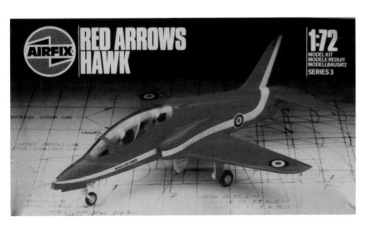

The arrangement with Heller proved, however, to be problematic. Heller undertook the production of kits for Airfix, and chronic problems with supplying the right volumes on time led to a major cash flow problem in 2006. The Airfix brand was still strong, and when the kits were able to reach the shops they sold well, but the business was forced into receivership once again.

This demise of Airfix was widely reported in the British media, the BBC2 *Newsnight* programme even ending its late night show with a time-lapsed sequence of a reporter building a 1:48 scale Spitfire. The popular story was that the Airfix name would disappear – that model making was an old-fashioned pastime unable to compete with the computer and game industry. This is a common argument, but other modelling companies were profitable, and the business pages always held the opinion that the Airfix brand was too strong not to survive. Revell again expressed an interest, but the British company Hornby eventually succeeded in acquiring both the Airfix and Humbrol brands.

The renaissance of Airfix under the management of Hornby – which in addition to its established railway model business also owns the famous Corgi and Scalextric brands – was nothing short of remarkable. All of the original Airfix moulds were returned from France, and were treated as a valued resource. Classics from the back catalogue started to reappear almost immediately, and parallel investments were made in a number of new kits.

The Sea Harrier was a topical kit from the early 1980s and one of the few originals produced by Airfix.

These kits were of an improved technical quality to compete with the high standards being set by competitors, but despite production being undertaken in the Far East, the design work was undertaken in England and the kits retained much of the classic Airfix style.

Some of the first kits commissioned by Hornby were based on the BBC television science fiction series *Dr Who*. A British institution, *Dr Who* fell out of favour and was 'rested' for sixteen years between 1989 and 2005. Eventually, it was reinvented with very high production values, and storylines that were stylish and 'edgy' in a way that appealed directly to young audiences. Linking the Airfix brand to this programme was a bold move. Equally bold was the use of the concept of an 'Airfix kit' and the Airfix brand in a bank advertising campaign. This campaign featured Lewis Hamilton, the first black Formula One champion, and made perfect use of the metaphor of an 'Airfix kit' to illustrate that a bank and the Formula One team it sponsored were the sum of many components that had to be brought together. The final indication that Airfix was back was the appearance of a 1:24 Mosquito fighter bomber in December 2009. This 'Superkit' was unfinished business for the brand, and with its appearance, Airfix moved confidently into the second decade of the twenty-first century.

The A10 'Tankbuster' was also a topical kit in the 1980s, but the kit, like many others in this period, was not an Airfix original. The moulds were designed by Heller in France.

THE AIRFIX STYLE: BOX ART AND PACKAGING

A LTHOUGH THE ORIGINAL Woolworths-inspired plastic bags and header cards were used until 1973, such packaging was only ever appropriate for small models. As soon as Airfix started to produce anything larger, boxes were required to protect the fragile and increasingly expensive contents. The concept behind the clear plastic bags – apart from economy of production costs – was that a prospective purchaser could see what his pocket money was about to buy. Even so, an illustration was required for the header card, and such illustrations became proportionately more important once the use of boxes became more common. With no contents on display, the box art became the means to sell the kit.

Until the early 1960s, the header cards and boxes were simply decorated with a line drawing of the subject in three or four colours. To modern eyes these designs look austere, but they made an impression on Woolworths shelves compared to the brown paper packaging and monocolour printing used on other products during this period. However, in the 1960s, Britain finally shed its post-war drabness with an explosion of colour in fashion, film and advertising. In a consumer society with an expanding economy, it was no longer good enough for a product simply to be on a shelf. Visual impact was needed, and to create this effect, Airfix decided to promote their kits via a style of dramatic, full-colour artwork.

A number of artists were commissioned to do this work, but two of the most accomplished were Roy Cross and Brian Knight. It is not an exaggeration to say that Cross and Knight produced some works of art for Airfix. Their paintings were almost photographically accurate representations, but the aircraft, tanks, cars and figures were placed in idealised situations that no photographer could ever have captured. The B-17 bomber box art painted by Roy Cross in 1963 is a perfect example of this style. The aircraft is visualised from below with bombs tumbling from an open bomb bay. German fighters are pressing home an attack, and one of the B-17's engines is trailing flames and black smoke. The B-17 is fighting back with its machine gun turrets blazing away into a blue sky crowded with

Opposite:
Box art and packaging styles have varied over the years, but the Airfix kit has always been distinctive.

Above: A rare surviving example of the first Airfix helicopter in its original bag packaging.

Below: The 'Blister' type packaging was a simple and effective updating of the traditional polythene bag used for smaller Series 1 kits. This well-preserved example contains the delightful de Havilland Chipmunk kit and dates from the early 1970s.

the white vapour trails of other aircraft. Airfix commissioned a unique piece of art for every single one of their kits. All were accurate, vivid and had the immediacy of what was to come years later (in a more clinical fashion) with computer-generated graphics.

Styles and tastes change, however. The polythene bags for Series 1 kits gave way in 1973 to a clear plastic tray moulded onto a stiff card. This 'blister pack' won a design award the following year, and retained the best feature of the polythene bags – being able to see the contents – within a much more robust package. Instructions were printed on the reverse of the header card, a large proportion of which was printed in colour. This gave scope for easier painting guidance – which was especially useful for kits such as the 54 mm Guardsman, which was one of the first to appear in this new form of packaging.

The style of the box art also began to change from the mid-1970s. New artwork tended to be airbrushed rather than painted in gouache – creating a more impressionistic and less vivid image. There were also fewer signs of offensive action. Changing public attitudes towards the imagery of war soon led to existing artwork being revised to remove all traces of violence. The classic B-17 painting for example had all traces of the burning engine, the falling bombs and machine gun fire removed.

The arrival of General Mills/Palitoy in the early 1980s led to the replacement of the artwork by

05005–0 Boeing B-17G Flying Fortress. This was the final and most successful version of the famous World War II bomber. The machine represented here is one the 447th Bombardment Group of the US 8th Air Force. The 100-part kit has a retractable undercarriage and many working features.

Classic Airfix box art. The Roy Cross painting of the B17 Flying Fortress in action was even more dramatic in the 1973 catalogue than on the kit box because a fuller depth of the canvas was used. The painting is so full of movement and sharp, cold danger that the viewer is almost tempted to duck.

close-up photography of assembled models. The rationale for this approach is said to be the legislation passed in some countries, requiring the actual contents of a box to be displayed on the outside. At the time, some other kit manufacturers followed the same guidance, and kit box art generally became less interesting for a number of years. However, other manufacturers such as Revell used expertly made models. Palitoy often used models made with less care and attention. Occasionally, the effect was so disappointing that it seemed as though the boxes had been designed by some of Airfix's competitors! All of this was puzzling, given the management theories held by General Mills concerning product impact. Possibly, they simply did not understand the product, and decided on the cheapest design standard to maximise profits.

The Swedish Draken was a futuristic design in the 1960s and inspired many of the aircraft in the *Thunderbirds* and *Captain Scarlet* television series. The Roy Cross illustration captures the shape and speed of the original aircraft as well as the Swedish landscape it normally flew over.

The General Mills/Palitoy era also saw an expansion of the languages used on instruction sheets. Early Airfix instruction sheets had been solely in English, and took the form of precise step-by-step written instructions next to a series of beautifully drawn assembly diagrams. This reflected the market Airfix's kits were sold in – Britain, the Commonwealth countries and, via a subsidiary called USAIRFIX, North America. In 1973 when Britain joined the Common Market, Airfix was looking for more export trade, and so modified its standard packaging and instruction leaflets. The latter lost the descriptive English text, which was replaced by more basic instructions in English,

Decal or transfers are a crucial part of any kit. Swastikas have not been included for German subjects since the 1970s. The image, associated with the Nazis, is banned in many European countries and in common with most kit manufacturers Airfix had to refrain from using the image.

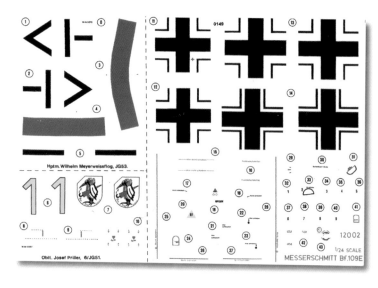

The original box art illustration for the T34 tank was extremely graphic in its portrayal of a scene from the Second World War.

French and German. The diagrams became more pictorial in nature, with the use of symbols for actions such as 'Cement', 'Do not Cement', 'Paint' and so on. Palitoy, however, moved this concept several steps further with many languages on an instruction sheet, which for some reason was often printed in blue ink!

The Humbrol period from the late 1980s through to 2006 saw a return to something similar to the classic Airfix style. The photographs were soon replaced by artwork: either a modified version of an original – violence still being discouraged – or a newly commissioned piece. This packaging style was a huge improvement on what had immediately preceded it, but it still

A good example of the 'USAirfix' packaging used for a while to make the products more appealing to the American market.

Typical Palitoy box art from the early 1980s.

lacked the edge of the 1960s, 1970s and the earlier periods, and the visual impact of some rival manufacturers.

In parallel with the changes in box art, the Airfix logo itself underwent some significant changes over the years. The now-familiar round, bright red Airfix logo was introduced in 1973 as part of the wider re-branding exercise that also gave rise to the blister packs for smaller kits. Before this, the Airfix logo had had two earlier and equally distinct styles. The first had been rectangular and is known as the 'angled ribbon' design. Until 1959, the word 'Airfix' was actually quite a small element in the logo, and had an equally prominent suffix, 'products in plastic' – an indication of the company's background. In 1959 the 'products in plastic' was dropped, and 'Airfix' expanded to fill the available space in the box. The background colour in the box during this period was also blue rather than red. In 1963, the box was stretched considerably and given a white background, and the space was used for black text, which typically read, 'Airfix 72 Scale'. This second style is often referred to as 'Red Stripe' because a red stripe was often added to the

The F84F Thunderstreak kit first appeared in 1974 with quite conservative decal options. In the 1990s the same kit was given a new lease of life with a striking option for the Italian Diavoli Rossi (Red Devils) aerobatic display team, which was vividly portrayed by a good example of the box art from this period.

Early style Hornby box art. A return to the more combative style of illustration which had been a hallmark of the brand in the 1960s and 1970s was quickly apparent.

The dramatic red-styled Hornby boxes introduced in 2009. The illustrations are computer generated and make the box tops more relevant to a modern audience familiar with the clarity and sharpness of imagery used in some computer games. The style, however, is still inescapably Airfix – the victorious Sea Harrier and shot down Argentinian Skyhawk being portrayed exactly as a scene from the Second World War would have been thirty years before.

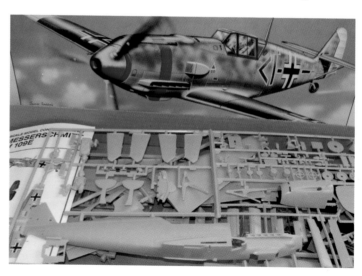

left of the box, although for a time different coloured stripes were used to denote the series of the particular kit.

The red circular logo has itself been modified over the years. Its design is effectively the angled ribbon logo highlighted by a red circular background.

The style was briefly changed between 1978 and 1981 to a red oval, which allowed the ribbon to be a little more prominent and more reminiscent of the older 1960s style. The oval was, however, short lived – as was a very messy version used between 1982 and 1983, which reduced the amount of red in the logo, removed the band and added 'Airfix Precision Model Kits'. In 1983, the more familiar modern style was introduced and this has been refined with the ribbons becoming more stylised – like lightning flashes – and in the Hornby period, the shade of red used becoming more vivid.

Hornby recognised the fact that red was associated with Airfix, and used the colour extensively in a major revamp of box design. Boxes became – depending upon your age – pillar-box or Red Arrows red, and were canvases for stunning computer-generated graphic designs. Full-colour inserts for painting guidance were also introduced for all kits, and the reluctance to portray war-like images was considerably relaxed. The artwork of the 1:24 scale Mosquito, which appeared in 2009, portrayed two aircraft engaged on the 1944 'Operation Jericho' Amiens prison raid mission. Bombs are not falling, but are exploding in the background. The image was confident and designed to fire the imagination. Airfix was back where it belonged.

Boxes full of pieces – the stuff of dreams.

BIBLIOGRAPHY

Carbonel, J. C. *The Airfix Toy Plastic Soldier*. Histoire & Collections, 2009.

Cross, Roy. *The Vintage Years of Airfix Box Art*. Crowood Press, 2009.

Graham, Thomas. *Remembering Revell Model Kits*. Schiffer, 2008.

Graham, Thomas. *Aurora Model Kits*. Schiffer, 2006.

Harley, Basil. *Constructional Toys*. Shire Publications, 1990.

Knight, Stephen. *Let's Stick Together: An Appreciation of Kitmaster and Airfix Railway Kits*. Irwell Press, 1999.

Lewarne, Pat. *The Enthusiasts' Guide to Airfix Models*. Collectakit, 1984.

Lines, Richard, and Heilstrom, Leif. *Frog Model Aircraft*. New Cavendish Books, 1994.

Ward, Arthur. *The Model World of Airfix*. Bellview Publishing, 1984.

Ward, Arthur. *Airfix: Celebrating 50 Years of the Greatest Plastic Kits in the World*. Harper Collins, 1999.

Ward, Arthur. *Classic Kits: Collecting the Greatest Kits in the World from Airfix to Tamiya*. Collins, 2004.

Ward, Arthur. *The Boys' Book of Airfix*. Ebury Press, 2009.

WEBSITES

www.airfix.com

www.airfixcollector.com

www.airfixtributeforum.com

www.youtube.com/watch?v=Xsx7af35TdM (the Lewis Hamilton advertisement)

www.airfixtoysoldiers.com

www.airfixrailways.co.uk

www.sworld.com.au/steven/models

www.airfix-usa.com

www.gregers.7.forumer.com

www.frogpenguin.com

The Airfix brand – enduring throughout the years.

INDEX

Page numbers in italics refer to illustrations